JEANNINE ATKINS

Mary Anning
and the Sea Dragon

Pictures by
MICHAEL DOOLING

*To Alen Guest —
my bcycfest wishes!
2016*

Library of Congress Cataloging-in-Publication Data
Atkins, Jeannine, date.
    Mary Anning and the sea dragon / Jeannine Atkins ; pictures by Michael Dooling.— 1st ed.
        p.   cm.
    Summary: An account of the finding of the first entire skeleton of an ichthyosaur, an extinct sea reptile, by a twelve-year-old
English girl who went on to become a paleontologist.
    ISBN-13: 978-1-480-05687-9
    ISBN-10: 1-480-05687-1
    1. Anning, Mary, 1799–1847—Juvenile literature.   2. Paleontology—England—Juvenile literature.   [1. Anning, Mary, 1799–1847—
Childhood and youth.   2. Paleontologists.   3. Fossils.   4. Women—Biography.]   I. Dooling, Michael, date, ill.   II. Title.
QE707.A56A74   1999
560'.92
[B]—DC21
                                                                                                                                97-47547

To Peter — J.A.

To Lou and Fran for their generosity — M.D.

The author and illustrator gratefully acknowledge Dr. John Maisey,
Fossil Fish Curator at the American Museum of Natural History,
New York, for his expert review of the text and illustrations

Mary Anning knew from the sound of the sea that the tide was going out. She was eager to search the shore for stone sea lilies and shells, but she had to watch her younger brothers while Mother worked.

Mary put more driftwood on the fire. Then she spoke slowly to her brothers as she made shadows of sea dragons on the wall. Getting to the end of a story quicker wouldn't bring her mother home any sooner.

But the minute her mother entered the cottage, Mary called their dog, Blackie, and grabbed her bonnet, basket, and tools. The sign reading GIFTS AND CURIOSITIES thudded against the door as Mother followed her outside, shouting, "Wait!"

Mother took Mary's straw bonnet and replaced it with a top hat.

"It's a gentleman's hat! It's not proper for a girl," Mary complained, repeating what her mother had said when Father was alive.

"It will keep your head safe from falling rocks, Mary," Mother said. That was what Father used to say. Sturdy top hats protected riders when they were flung from their horses. Mother tucked a flower into Mary's hatband and whispered, "Someday you'll wear the finest hat in town."

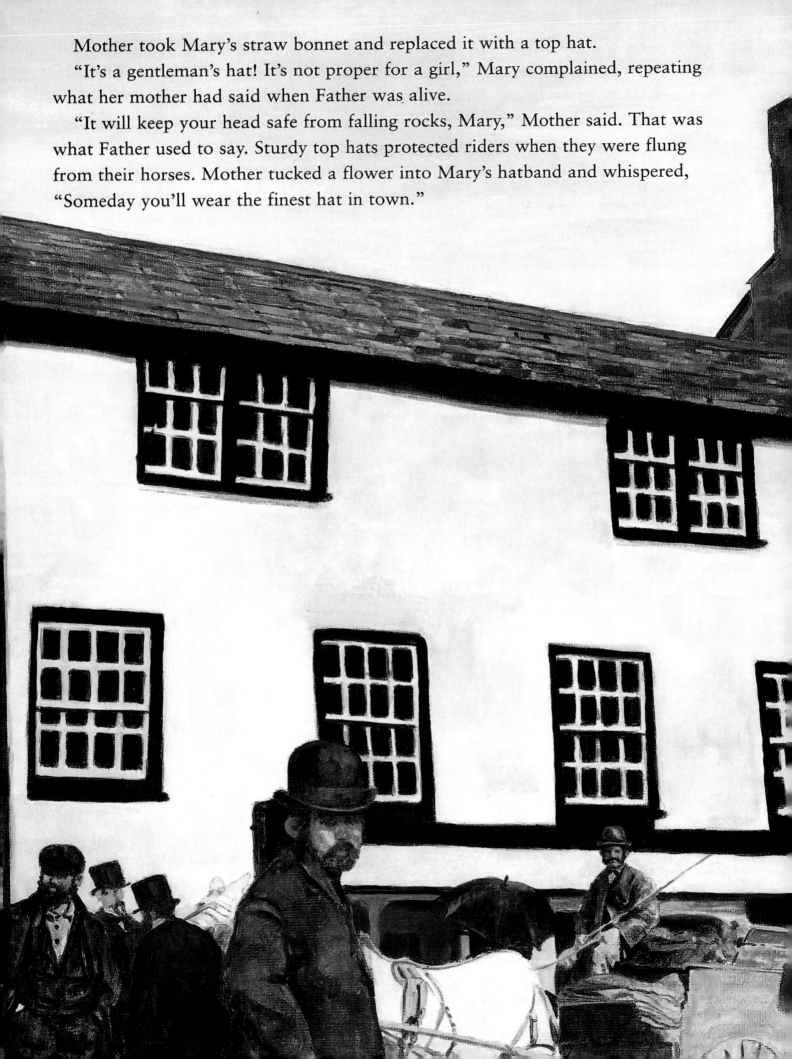

Mary kissed her mother goodbye and raced down to the seashore. When she reached the blue-gray cliffs, she raised her arms to feel the breeze beneath them, imagining that she was flying. Then she set to work, looking along the beach for stone curiosities and shells to sell to the people from the city who came here for the sea air.

After Mary's father had died last year, when she was ten, Mary quit school to help earn money. Mother sold most of Father's carpentry tools to buy food. The saw and measures were gone, but Mary would never forget the way Father had walked with her through the woods so that she'd know where his chairs and tables had come from. "Everything starts from something living," he'd said. "If you look hard, you can see the tree that's in a table."

So Mary looked hard, as usual. She climbed over stones that the rain and wind had broken from the cliffs. She looked until she spotted some markings on a wide, flat stone. She chipped with her chisel and hammer. The lines seemed to form a tooth. She'd found teeth before. The tourists rarely bought them. Mary marked the spot and moved on to look for something prettier.

Before long, Mary found a snakestone. Its outline was as faint as a shadow. She chiseled away the softer stone around it, brushed off the dust, cut the snakestone from the rock, and dropped it into her basket. Then she straightened her back, looking at the cliffs where her father had fallen. The fall had worsened the cough Father died from, but he'd never hated the cliffs or the storms that loosened the rocks. There was something in the broken stones that he'd been searching for. "Don't ever stop looking, Mary," he used to say.

Mary hurried back to the spot she had marked. What if there wasn't just one tooth but a row of them? Mary chipped gently. Another shape like the first appeared. Mary was certain now that these were teeth, but of what creature? A wave touched her skirt, warning her that it was time to leave the beach. Once the tide swept in, there was nowhere to stand between the cliffs and the cold, fierce sea.

During the following weeks, Mary hunted for curiosities to sell. She also spent part of each day chiseling stone from a row of teeth that was growing longer and longer. Above the sound of the waves she heard her tapping and brushing, then a hush while she examined what she'd uncovered. Finally, a face about four feet long emerged from beneath her hands and knees.

Mary brought her family to see it.

"Ugh, a crocodile!" her cousin Sarah said.

"What would a crocodile be doing in England?" asked Mary's older brother, Joseph. "It's a sea dragon!"

"Even if there's more to this sea dragon and she can get it out, who on earth would want it in their parlor?" Aunt Ruth frowned. "People already gossip about the way Mary runs around with a hammer and chisel and that silly hat. Her skirts are soaked."

"Clothing dries," Mary's mother said.

"When is she going to stop?" Aunt Ruth demanded.

"I expect she'll stop when she's finished." Mother squeezed Mary's hand. She seemed to know that Mary couldn't leave this etched stone any more than a nurse could turn from a patient, or an artist abandon a half-finished painting.

All winter, Mary worked with chapped, red hands. Her cloak flapped in the wind. *Don't ever stop looking, Mary.* Examining the shapes of bones, Mary heard her father's voice as clearly as if he were speaking to her now.

Spring arrived, and a backbone emerged. Then a wing, or was it a fin or a paddle? The more Mary worked, the more she wondered: How long ago was long ago? What was here before us?

One June night, Mary's mother answered a knock at the cottage door.

"I'd like to speak to Miss Anning." A gentleman took off his tall hat and glanced into the shop. "I'm Lord Henley. My family's here on holiday, and some children took me to see what they call a sea dragon. Is it true that the lady who found it lives here?"

"You must want my daughter." Mother proudly nodded at Mary.

The gentleman looked surprised to find himself facing a girl who'd just turned twelve. Then he smiled and said, "Fossils are an interest of mine, too."

"Fossils?" Mary said.

"Fossils are traces of old life left in stone. What you call curiosities," Lord Henley explained. "Do you know what it is you've found, miss?"

"No, sir. Do you?"

"All I know is that it must be thousands of years old. Maybe millions. We can learn a lot about the earth from something like this," Lord Henley said. "I'll give you ten pounds for it now and another ten when you get it out. That thing is already bigger than any of us, but I expect you'll find a way to pry it out. You seem to know your trade."

Encouraged by the prospect of more money than the Anning family had ever had, Joseph took time off from his job at a quarry to help Mary. But his hands were used to hammering hard and fast. His fingers were too rough to feel the slight impressions in the stone.

Some friends also wanted to help and borrowed tools from the blacksmith and stonemasons. But they found the work dull.

Soon Mary worked alone again. She remained alert to changes in the stone's hardness, listening when her hammer hit the chisel. A faint sound told her to alter the chisel's angle or she risked cracking the part of the rock that she was trying to save.

In one day she usually exposed an area half the size of her hand. But Mary forgot her own time as millions of the earth's years fell away.

Late in the summer, almost a year after she'd begun, Mary worked with Joseph and some of his friends to remove the fossil from the surrounding stone. They cut the creature into slabs, which they carried on blankets to a horse and wagon.

Almost everyone in town came to watch. Tourists peered over one another's shoulders as much to see Mary as to see the fossil.

Lord Henley shook Mary's hand. He said, "Nothing like this has ever been found in England."

"At least you're done with that, Mary," Aunt Ruth said. "Now will you settle down to a normal life?"

Mary touched the fossil for courage, the way she had once reached for her mother's hand. There were creatures no one had ever thought existed. There were worlds no one had ever dreamed of. "I have work to do," Mary said.

Later, Mary watched the horse and wagon pull the fossil past the shops on Broad Street. Someday maybe she would go to London to see it displayed in a museum. She'd buy a splendid bonnet for her mother, but she'd keep her tall black hat. And she'd return to this shore to look for fossils, to hear the wind and her father's voice: *Don't ever stop looking, Mary.*

AFTERWORD

Eleven years after finding what we now call an ichthyosaur, Mary Anning dug out the fossil of another sea reptile. It was the first plesiosaur to be found in England. Among her other important discoveries was a fossilized pterosaur, an extinct flying reptile.

Throughout her life, Mary continued to excavate and study fossils, becoming one of the first persons to make a living at this work. Unlike most of the women of her time, she never married. Instead, she kept and expanded her father's store, where she always sold stone sea lilies (fossils of leafy, flowerlike marine animals) and snakestones (the coiled fossil shells of extinct marine mollusks, which we now call ammonites). She enjoyed the friendship and respect of many well-known scientists.

Mary Anning lived to see the word "dinosaur" coined in 1841. After her death, she was honored with a stained-glass window in the church in Lyme Regis, England, where she spent her entire life (May 21, 1799–March 9, 1847). Many of the fossils she uncovered are still studied and exhibited in museums.

Today some scientists believe that only people with special training should be allowed to dig out fossils. But many paleontologists speak gratefully of the children and amateur rock collectors whose findings have raised and answered important questions about the earth. They ask, "Where would we be today without Mary Anning?"

Made in the USA
Charleston, SC
23 October 2015